FENG SHUI

DOs & TABOOs
for LOVE

ANGI MA WONG

FENG SHUI

DOs & TABOOs

for LOVE

Hay House, Inc.
Carlsbad, California • Sydney, Australia
Canada • Hong Kong • United Kingdom

CONTENTS

A PERSONAL MESSAGE

I'T'S BEEN THRILLING TO EXPERIENCE THE PHENOMENAL success of my bestselling book *Feng Shui Dos & Taboos,* both in its original and gift versions. Thank you for raving about it and recommending it to so many others, thus contributing to its extraordinary popularity. Once again, I'm delighted to share my Chinese heritage with you—in an easy-to-understand and user-friendly format—to help you achieve your goals.

Many of you have corresponded with me to describe the positive changes that feng shui has brought to your lives, thus validating the power of this wonderful knowledge. And my sincere appreciation goes to those of you who have committed yourselves (as I have) to maintaining the cultural integrity of feng shui by keeping it close and true to its Chinese roots. "When you drink the water, remember its source" is an old Chinese proverb that reminds us to practice feng shui with respect and reverence for the culture from which it originates, as well as with pure hearts and strong intentions.

IN MY TRAVELS AROUND THE GLOBE—FROM ISTANBUL TO Illinois, from New Zealand to New England—unequivocally, there are three universal things that people desire the most in their lives: love, good health, and wealth. I'm delighted to focus on the first topic in this book. And since I've been married to my husband, Norman, for 35 years, I feel very qualified to pen this book.

*"The best and most beautiful things in the world
cannot be seen or even touched.
They must be felt with the heart."*
— HELEN KELLER

WITHIN A FEW MINUTES OF OUR MEETING AT A CHINESE NEW Year celebration, I had the attractive banker in the expensive suit pegged as a type-A personality—intelligent, focused, aggressive . . . a typical woman warrior.

"Many men come in and out of my life," she confided during our consultation, "but I quickly get bored with them. However, I'm in my 30s, and I want to marry and settle down. Give me one quick tip on how I can achieve this."

As she spoke, she showed me around her bachelorette bedroom, and I noticed the location of the doorway.

"Tell you what," I said. "I'll give you two. Your bedroom door in your marriage area represents the men in your life coming in and out. Keep your bedroom door closed all the time, except when you're using it, and tie two red ribbons on the inside doorknob."

Two years later, I bumped into the banker again.

"I've been meaning to contact you all this time!" she said. "Within a month of doing what you suggested, I met the man I married, and we have a baby girl!"

LOVE IS THE STUFF OF DREAMS, DRAMA, AND DREAD, AS WELL as agony and ecstasy. And yet who among us can live without it? Scientific research has shown that both plants and people perish without attention and care.

The pages that follow will concentrate on providing tips on attracting many different kinds of relationships—not just the romantic or passionate kinds. After all, we experience the love of our families long before that of friends, lovers, mates, or partners. Love blossoms from the seeds of harmony, kindness, communication, commitment, respect, affection, and growth.

Feng shui must be practiced in concert with your spiritual, emotional, physical, and intellectual development. Just like the legs on a table, all of these aspects of your well-being contribute to your being centered or grounded. And without your active involvement in creating your own luck, your efforts and intentions will be weakened and less successful. Romance means that you must take risks to become involved with another person . . . so read on!

I dedicate this newest work to *you,* so that through feng shui, you can energize both your relationships and your life.

Best wishes,
Angi Ma Wong

www.FengShuiLady.com
www.AsianConnections.com
e-mail: amawong@worldnet.att.net

INTRODUCTION

FENG SHUI BELONGS TO A HOLISTIC PHILOSOPHY THAT encompasses chi gong, tai chi, acupuncture, acupressure, martial arts, herbs, tonics, and the many practices associated with traditional Chinese medicine (TCM). All of these pursuits share the same three basic concepts: energy flow, balance and harmony, and the five elements.

First, there is what's known as *chi* in the Mandarin dialect or *hey* in the Cantonese dialect spoken in Southern China, Hong Kong, and Singapore (and by the old-timers of the world's Chinatowns). Chi defines the cosmic energy or aura that emanates and surrounds *all* things, be they organic or inorganic. Chi is water, wind, the sun's rays, a person's spirit, magnetic fields, and the multitude of energy forms that exist. Sometimes chi is visible and sometimes it isn't. We cannot see the sun's rays or the wind, only the manifestations of their power. We cannot see the magnetism of the earth's poles or the moon's gravitational pull, but we see how the world's climate and tides change.

In feng shui and TCM, beneficial chi always flows in wavy or curved lines, like the wind and water in nature. A meandering stream is fast enough to remain a fresh source of water, but slow enough to create still pools for fish and add enriching soil to its inside curves. Very few instances of perfectly straight lines occur in nature, except in short segments. One example is the straight stalk between the canes in a bamboo or sugar plant. Almost all other straight lines that exist in the world are man-made, and are consequently considered un-natural. For example, when river water travels along a straight path, it's at its fastest and most powerful, destroying or killing everything in its way. To describe this destructive energy, the Chinese use the word *sha* (which literally means "to kill") as a modifier in front of chi, creating *sha chi*, meaning "killing energy." However, sha chi doesn't translate to "poison arrow" as some other feng shui books have stated.

Good feng shui promotes and creates positive air and traffic flow—in both interior and exterior environments—by avoiding the killing energies created by straight lines and their convergence, such as the corners of buildings, roads, tunnels, streets, and so forth.

The second fundamental concept of feng shui is that of balance. The familiar symbol of the tai chi (also known as the yin/yang symbol) literally means "ultimate energy," as it evolved from the Chinese idea of the origin of the universe. In the beginning, there was chaos, with air and earth swirling around, until eventually, the heavier particles settled and clumped together, creating planet Earth and clearing the skies to create the heavens.

Figure A –
The Tai Chi Symbol

The tai chi symbol also represents the duality of the universe and everything in it—the yin and the yang. Yin, meaning "dark," is the feminine half: soft, negative, passive, and nurturing. Yang means "light," and it's the masculine half: hard, positive, and aggressive. The yin and yang are *not* opposites of each other; rather, they're halves of a whole, with the *S* line between them moving, depending on the balance of the two. This symbol also reminds us that when the yang is at its zenith, it begins its transformation into yin, and vice versa, in much the same way as midnight is the beginning of a day, and noon is the beginning of night. Note that the tai chi design has a dot of the yin in the yang half, and a dot of the yang in the yin: The Chinese realized thousands of years ago that every man had a bit of the female within him, and the female had a bit of the male. Today, that idea has become a familiar expression said to men: "Get in touch with your feminine side."

The third major idea in both feng shui and TCM is that of the five elements: wood, fire, earth, metal, and water. They relate to each other in two different ways, generative and destructive. In the generative relationship, one element is the source for the next; while in the destructive cycle, an element can destroy another. There's nothing superstitious or metaphysical about these relationships—in fact, you can see them at work in nature.

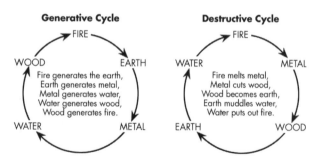

Generative Cycle

FIRE

WOOD   EARTH

Fire generates the earth,
Earth generates metal,
Metal generates water,
Water generates wood,
Wood generates fire.

WATER   METAL

Destructive Cycle

FIRE

WATER   METAL

Fire melts metal,
Metal cuts wood,
Wood becomes earth,
Earth muddles water,
Water puts out fire.

EARTH   WOOD

Figure B – The Generative and Destructive Element Cycles

Most of us understand how wood creates a fire, fire creates earth (a volcano's lava produces new land), earth creates metal, metal generates water (water appears on a metal surface from condensation), and water nourishes wood (all plant life).

On the other hand, plants (wood) deplete earth in order to grow, earth will hold back water (in a dam), water extinguishes fire, fire melts down metal, and metal (in the form of pruning shears, axes, and saws) cuts down wood.

These three concepts are interrelated and complementary, serving as the foundation for feng shui.

FIVE COMPONENTS OF DESTINY

In Chinese thought, feng shui is only one of the five components that make up our destinies. The other four are fate, luck, charity, and education.

Fate represents all the circumstances of our birth: where, when, which family, birth order, ethnicity, socio-economic circumstances, and so on. Luck consists of three different kinds: man-made, pure, and heaven. Then comes feng shui, the ancient Chinese environment system of aligning human energies with that of nature and the universe. Next is charity and philanthropy: doing good deeds and creating good karma through one's thoughts and actions. Last is education and self-development, as we should always be stretching our minds, bodies, and spirits to higher levels.

FENG SHUI SCHOOLS

More than 4,000 years ago, people in China began to practice *geomancy,* the knowledge of the rhythms and energy lines of the earth. For many millennia, that knowledge, called *feng* (wind) and *shui* (water) was kept secret by the emperors to maintain their power and control over their millions of subjects. Form School is generally accepted as being the original feng shui—practitioners studied and evaluated the geography of the land forms surrounding a client's property and assigned specific attributes to them that governed their life.

Form School practitioners apprenticed under the tutelage of masters, who, in turn, studied under grand masters. The meaning of the title "master" can range in meaning from simply one's "teacher" to the most learned of those who possess superior feng shui skills supported by decades of study and practical experience.

With the Chinese invention of the compass, feng shui became a more exacting art, complete with complex formulas, a plethora of water and land-form combinations, and vast knowledge and observations recorded and written by grand masters who had preceded each generation.

It's been said that there have been more than 30 forms of feng shui. But today, two schools appear to dominate the English-speaking world: traditional Compass School and Black Sect. Both transpose the octagon called the *bagua* on various rooms to determine what to place where within a space, and both assign different aspects of one's life to the various areas of a room. But they do these things in dramatically different fashions.

Even though I'm a classically trained, traditional Compass School practitioner, I've actually been practicing, writing, and teaching an integrated form of feng shui for many years, and I'm happy to share that information with you in this book.

THE COMPASS SCHOOL

In the Compass School, which is about 3,000 years old and practiced all over the world, a compass (Chinese or Western) is used to identify a space's magnetic North first, after which the remaining seven directions fit into place: North is always North in a room, office, or garden; South is always South, and so forth. The compass directions are fixed and constant, and the bagua map subsequently matches the eight zones formed by a grid placed over a space. All eight areas are associated with different aspects of one's life and with the eight cardinal and secondary compass directions of N, NE, E, SE, S, SW, W, and NW.

The following list explains the eight compass directions and what they represent in the Compass School:

- **North (N):** Career and business success; black; winter; water element generated by metal; tortoise; the number 1

- **Northeast (NE):** Love of learning; spiritual, intellectual, mental, and emotional growth; turquoise, blue, or green; winter becoming spring; earth element generated by fire; the number 8

- **East (E):** Family, harmony, health, and prosperity; new beginnings; green, black, or blue; spring; wood element generated by water; water; dragon; the number 3

- **Southeast (SE):** Wealth, prosperity, and abundance; green or purple; spring becoming summer; wood element generated by water; water; the number 4

- **South (S):** Fame and fortune; longevity; festivity and joy; red; summer; fire element generated by wood; bird; the number 9

- **Southwest (SW):** Love, marriage, romance, relationships, and spouses; teamwork; gold, yellow, red, pink, or white; summer becoming autumn; earth element generated by fire; the number 2

- **West (W):** Children; creativity; white or silver; autumn; metal element generated by earth; earth; tiger; the number 7

- **Northwest (NW):** Father; helpful people, mentors, and benefactors; interests outside the home; trade; travel; gray, white, or yellow; autumn becoming winter; metal element; earth; the number 6

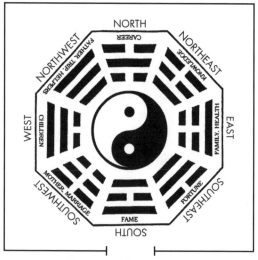

Figure C – The Bagua Map

Dir.	Color	Animal	No.	Element	Season
N	Black, blue	Tortoise	1	Water	Winter
NE	Turquoise		8	Earth	Winter to Spring
E	Green, blue	Dragon	3	Wood	Spring
SE	Green, purple		4	Wood	Spring to Summer
S	Red, purple	Phoenix	9	Fire	Summer
SW	Yellow, pink, red		2	Earth	Summer to Fall
W	White, metallic	Tiger	7	Metal	Fall
NW	Grey, metallic		6	Metal	Fall to Winter

Figure D – Compass School Directions

THE BLACK SECT SCHOOL

The Black Sect Tantric Tibetan Buddhist School of feng shui has been popularized in the United States in the last several years, although its roots trace back to Buddhism. This school doesn't need or use a compass at all. As in the Compass School, the bagua octagon governs certain aspects of one's life, but these are called "aspirations" or goals. What distinguishes this form of feng shui from others is that the bagua rotates, room by room, depending on where the main entrance is. For instance, the center of the wall where the main entrance is located is always the Career area.

The Black Sect School also relies greatly on its "Nine Cures": wind chimes and bells; crystals; mirrors; lights; plants and flowers; aquariums and fishbowls; moving or powered objects; heavy objects; and bamboo flutes.

The following diagram shows how the aspirations fit into a space:

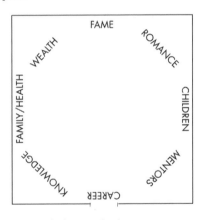

Figure E – Black Sect School Rotating Bagua Map

The list below describes what each area of a room represents according to the Black Sect School:

- **Front Center** (at the entrance looking into the room): Career; black or white; fountains; water

- **Left Front:** Knowledge, self-development, and success; personal goals and health; blue, black, or green; books

- **Left Center:** Family and ancestors; health; blue or green; heirlooms; shrines; photos

- **Left Rear:** Wealth, prosperity, abundance, and material things of value; red, purple, blue, or green; fountains, aquariums, and fish; banners

- **Center Rear** (across from main entrance): Fame and fortune; red or green; candles and fireplaces; awards and diplomas

- **Right Rear:** Marriage, relationships, spouse, and romance; mother; yellow

- **Right Center:** Children and creativity; white; metal; arts and crafts, toys, and games

- **Right Front:** Friends and supportive and helpful people; travel; father; black, white, or gray; religious icons

Take a few minutes to compare and understand the differences between these two popular forms of feng shui, and then choose the one that feels right for you. Whichever it is, be consistent and use common sense. You've probably figured out that you can't mix these two forms of feng shui because where you place your enhancements will differ significantly from the Compass School to the Black Sect School.

HOW TO USE FENG SHUI TO ATTRACT LOVE

By consulting the above, you can see where you should place items according to the two schools. Years ago, I created the acronym CANE to help friends and clients remember what to place where. The letters represent: (C)olor, (A)nimal symbol, (N)umber, and (E)lement. By putting the right CANEs in the right place, you'll stimulate the energy in that area.

Also keep in mind both the generative and destructive relationships of the elements so that what you do supports and doesn't destroy your feng shui efforts. For example, knowing that in the Compass School, SW is the prime direction for activating romance, love, and marriage, you should then avoid using any wood here because wood destroys the element of earth (SW).

Notice that good relationships can be achieved by stimulating several areas in each room, not just the romance areas. After all, you wouldn't want to undermine your efforts by loading up the SW (Compass) or right rear (Black Sect) zones to the exclusion of other aspects. For the purposes of this book, you'll notice that I mainly focus on the SW, NW, E, NW, and W areas. But, above all else, *keep balance and moderation in mind*, even in the bedroom, where a large number of dos and taboos apply.

> *"Some people change jobs, mates, and friends,*
> *but never think of changing themselves."*
> — JOHN C. MAXWELL

As you search for romance, keep in mind that feng shui won't do the job all by itself. Before you spend time, money, and energy on looking for that ideal romantic partner, take a good look at *yourself*. Begin by making (or remaking) yourself into the kind of person that you'd like to have a relationship with—only then can you develop into a person someone else would love, for feng shui is as much about changing the *person inside* as it is about changing his or her *environment outside.*

Remember to practice feng shui with a pure heart and strong intentions. Gladly use this wonderful ancient knowledge to your advantage and personal enrichment, but don't practice it to harm anyone. This means that it's acceptable to strengthen your position in someone else's life with feng shui, but to use it to eliminate your competition for that person's affections creates bad karma and will surely backfire.

You should also keep a feng shui journal or diary that records the things you did to change the feng shui in your life to attract love, and the dates you did them. Follow up by recording the results.

In conclusion, remember the "3 Golden Rules of the Feng Shui Lady":

1. **If it isn't broken, don't fix it.** Ask yourself if you're happy, healthy, and prosperous: If the answers are yes, yes, and yes, then only fine-tune or make minor changes in your life. You don't want to make major overhauls and upset the blessings and good things you already have.

2. **If you don't see it, it isn't there.** Feng shui is a mental, practical, metaphysical, and spiritual process that uses a range of strategies, including assessment, addition, camouflage, removal, deflection, transformation, and protection.

3. **Everything is fixable.** Feng shui offers hope, empowerment, and a marvelous opportunity for taking charge and being proactive to change your life.

Now, discover a treasure trove of feng shui dos and taboos for enhancing love in your life!

31

DOs & TABOOs
for LOVE

Don't set up an altar for a deceased spouse or sweetheart in your romance area.

Do create a special
place in your home
for a loved one if you
don't have mementos
of that person.

Do put your religious altars or memorials in rooms other than your bedroom.

Don't place a second-story bed directly above a room that has an altar.

Do put your religious or family altars in a quiet place, rather than in a heavily trafficked area in your home.

Don't put an altar to a deity next to, over, or across from your bed.

Don't use images of two animals of the same gender in your décor— pair a male with a female.

Do place figurines of dogs in your home, as they represent faithfulness.

Do hang a picture of a female tiger with her cubs in the W to improve your relationship with your children.

44

Do have a pair of Chinese lions or fu dogs gracing the exterior entrance of your home for protection.

Don't fill your bed with stuffed animals—this leaves no room for a new love interest.

Don't wear antique wedding rings from an estate sale, pawnshop, or people you don't know. They may have retained negative, unhappy, or unlucky energy from their former owners.

Don't locate an aquarium near the right side of the main entrance of your home facing out.

Do properly bury the ashes of a loved one.

Don't keep
the ashes of a
loved one in
your bedroom.

Don't put symbols of love or romance in a bathroom, which has the killing energy of human waste.

Do sleep on a "real" bed
(elevated off the floor)
to permit beneficial and
healthful chi energy to
circulate around you as
you sleep.

Don't keep or use the mattress or bed from a previous or failed marriage—buy a new one to symbolize a new beginning.

Don't use a headboard that has sharp or pointed metal pieces in its design.

53

Don't line up the end
of your bed directly
with either the bedroom
or bathroom door:
This is considered the
death position and is
very inauspicious.

Don't install any mirrors on the ceiling or behind the head-board of your bed, for the images will disturb the recharging of your energies.

Do be sure
that there's a
headboard on
your bed to pro-
vide support for
your aspirations.

Do match the material of your headboard with the element of its compass direction.

Do attach an opaque material behind a headboard (if it has an open design) to create support for you as you sleep.

Do sleep on the side of the bed that's farthest from the bedroom entrance if you want more influence in your home.

Don't sleep in a bunk bed because the energy of the ceiling or upper bunk will push down on you.

Don't sleep in a canopy-covered bed, as it restricts healthful chi from moving around you.

Don't choose a bed that has wooden or metal posts at its corners—especially if they have pointed ends—as these emanate killing energy to the bed's occupants.

Do take care that there are no corners of furniture (such as a dresser or bookshelves) that point toward your bed. These edges send out sha energy, causing poor health.

Do use soft, curving lines and designs in your bed linens to attract good rest.

Do try to place your bed in the dominant energy area of the room: diagonally across from its main entrance. This position will empower you while you're sleeping.

Don't put the head of your bed on a wall that has bathroom plumbing on the other side of it.

Don't sleep in a bed that has a door opening toward the pillows from the sides.

Don't install ceiling fans directly over the bed; instead, place them past the foot of the bed.

Do cleanse and purify any antique beds or furniture outdoors before you bring them into your home.

Don't use the space under the bed for storage—things there will block good chi flow to the bed's occupants.

Don't sleep with your head close to electrical outlets, as these are sources of much unhealthful sha chi.

Do be certain that you or your bedmate can get into bed from both sides.

Do cover up open electrical outlets near your pillow with plastic childproof plugs or heavy tape.

Don't "float" your bed in the center of your bedroom—there will be no support for you and your goals, from any direction.

Don't have your
bed facing a window
because it admits
too much yang energy
in the form of light,
heat, and uncomfort-
able glare.

Don't place your bed
behind the entrance
door to the room,
as this is a position
to which chi cannot
easily flow or reach.

Don't put the head of your bed against a wall that has the kitchen stove on the other side.

Do store bed linens, towels, pillows, blankets, and other sleep-related items in a bed that has drawers underneath it.

Don't have your head under a beam, alcove, track lighting, or lower ceiling when you're sleeping. These all press the energy down and make you susceptible to headaches.

Do replace the linens and pillows on your bed after the breakup of a relationship.

Don't store weapons, guns, swords, and the like under your bed.

Do choose a bed that's off the floor—rather than a sofa or futon, which represents an impermanent situation.

Do choose bed linens of natural fabrics, such as silk, cotton, and linen.

Don't let your children sleep on the floor.

Don't use bed linens with dark colors such as black or gray—they resemble tomblike conditions or being buried, which is definitely very yin and inauspicious. Instead, use white or pastels.

Do change the position of the bed when your romance has ended.

Don't fill your bed with pillows or animals (stuffed or live). Leave room for someone to share it!

Do mist your sheets and pillows with a scented spray before you retire for the night, as the aroma will increase sensuality and serenity.

Do create a bedroom that will recharge your physical, spiritual, sexual, and emotional energies.

Do decorate with yin and yang in mind: darker flooring materials, lighter-colored walls, and ceilings in the lightest hues.

Don't use any preserved or dead flowers or plants in your bedroom.

Don't have too many straight lines in your bedroom—instead, create balance with curves, arches, and circular shapes.

Do put a love-seat in the SW area of your bedroom for snuggling.

Do display seven photos or pictures of children in metal frames in the W of your bedroom to promote an addition to your family.

Don't position your bed under a beam that comes between you and your partner.

Do put images of a pair of doves in the relationship area in your bedroom to attract love and romance around you.

Don't sleep in a bedroom next to a kitchen if you're the head of your household. This area puts you at greater risk of fire and disturbs your peace of mind.

97

Do minimize the use of synthetic materials in your bedroom. Use natural fibers as much as you can for good health.

Do avoid geometric shapes, especially triangles, in your bedroom linens and décor—these shapes emanate negative sha energy.

99

Don't let any part of your body be reflected in a bedroom mirror, as this disturbs your rest.

Do use red as an accent color to increase passion in your bedroom.

101

Do keep your bedroom free of clutter to allow beneficial chi to flow freely there.

Do put a pair of chopsticks tied with red cord in the SW corner of your bedroom if you desire children. They mean "fast children" in Chinese!

Don't sleep in a bedroom over a garage, as the fumes and vibrations disturb sleep and health.

104

Do look at the view that you wake up to with a critical eye, and make feng shui changes if necessary.

Don't use
your bedroom
for an office.

Do use an opaque drape or partition to block the view of an opening without a door.

Do remove all exercise equipment from your bedroom.

Do separate the work and sleep areas of your loft or studio apartment.

Don't fill your bed-room with books, toys, statues, and other nonsleeping items.

Do keep your sleeping area a very personal and private area, away from guests and children.

Don't get in the habit of allowing your children or pets to share your bedroom.

Do see your bedroom
as a refuge where
you can recuperate
from the troubles
and cares of the
outside world.

Don't allow your bedroom to become another family room that's populated by your home's other occupants.

Do preserve the intimacy of your bedroom—allow others in by invitation only.

Don't keep photographs of a deceased spouse or partner in your bedroom.

Do keep your laundry, medicine bottles, and other distracting objects out of sight of the bedroom.

Don't use bright lights in your bedroom, as they're too yang.

Do create a sensual mood in your bedroom with lighting, textures, and colors.

Do close your bedroom drapes or shutters at night.

Don't overdecorate with too many flowers (either alive or images) in your bedroom.

Do display the
Chinese character for
"Double Happiness"
in your home,
especially in the
bedroom.

DOUBLE HAPPINESS

DOUBLE HAPPINESS

LOVE

Don't sleep in
a bedroom that
has power lines
attached outside
its wall.

Don't have a bar, refrigerator, or fireplace in your bedroom. These energies are too yang and disturb the quieting yin energy that recharges your "internal batteries."

Do sleep with all doors into your bedroom closed, especially those that lead to a bathroom.

Don't sleep in a bedroom that's adjacent to your parents'.

Don't make a room with irregularly angled walls your bedroom. Such angles represent imbalance and disturb the smooth circulation of beneficial chi.

129

Do keep your bedroom furniture, accessories, and décor simple and restful.

Do keep your bedroom dust and dirt free for better rest.

Do create a "female-friendly" bedroom if you're a man.

Do hang pictures of apple blossoms in the E to bring a beautiful woman into your life.

Do decorate with peach in your bed-room if you're a single woman, for this is the color that attracts a good man.

Don't design your bedroom so that it's overly feminine if you want to attract a man into your life.

Do add images of men and/or couples to your walls if you're a single woman.

Don't illuminate the NW corner of any room, as this may attract untrustworthy men into your life.

Do decorate with images of the Chinese phoenix in your bedroom if you're a single woman. This is one of the traditional symbols for marriage.

Do use pink or peach-colored candles in the SW area of your bedroom if you're a single woman. The fire element will give your romance and relationship area a boost.

141

Don't move, dust, or clean under a pregnant woman's bed until after her child's birth. To do so may dislodge or harm the baby's essential life force.

Don't

Do be mindful that the bedroom is the most intimate place for couples, including their thoughts and dreams.

Do teach your children and their friends to respect the privacy of your bedroom and to knock and wait for permission to enter.

Don't allow your children to enter your bedroom without your permission.

Do assign bedrooms in the W or NE to your children.

Don't decorate with primary colors in children's bedrooms—these yang colors tend to overstimulate.

Do use yin colors of blue and green to calm down over-active children.

Do place a figur-
ine or painting of a
pheasant or phoenix
in the S of any room
for happiness and
marriage.

Do use paint-
ings of a pair of
magpies in your
decorating, as
they mate for
life.

Do decorate with a pair of cranes (which represent long life) for the couple that heads up a family.

Do put books about fatherhood in the NW, motherhood/raising children and marriage in the SW, and family relationships in the E.

Do light red candles in multiples of two in the SW of your bedroom.

Don't put lights or candles in the NW area of your rooms because the fire element destroys the mentoring and bene-factor aspects of that direction.

155

Do install outdoor candles in the S and SW areas of your garden to add the generating energy of fire to your earth-related love relationships.

Do avoid placing your bed under a ceiling fan.

Don't place your bed at the short wall of a pitched ceiling.

Don't

158

Don't choose a bedroom with pitched, high, or cathedral ceilings.

Do group and light yellow or red candles at the center of your home to "keep the home fires burning."

Do think "Mother Earth" if you desire children, and add earth, clay, porcelain, or china to your home.

Do use images of tigers at rest in the W if you want to add children to your family. Tigers represent the direction of West and children.

Do place a metal elephant in the W to enhance your children energy.

163

Don't hang on to belongings, furnishings, gifts, and mementos from an unsuccessful relationship.

Do conduct an energy cleansing with a lighted acupuncturist's moxibustion stick by passing it near the walls in each room when you move into a new home.

Don't buy wedding rings or gowns from a divorced person.

Do use pink candles in multiples of two in the SW of your bedroom.

Do add more red
to your home to
stimulate loving
feelings.

Do use lots of lavender and violet if you love feeling and being more spiritual.

Do decorate the NW area of your home with white, gray, or silver accessories to enhance love between you and your father.

Do add pink to your bedroom, especially if you're a single woman.

Don't wear a green hat or cap if you're a man because it means that your wife or sweetheart is unfaithful to you.

Do keep blue and black out of the S part of your rooms or garden.

Do add red or deep purple judiciously to your bedroom to increase passion.

Do add more
yellow to your
home to stimulate
the "grounding"
of its occupants.

Do use yellow in your SW bathroom to dam the disturbance of water in your relationship area.

Don't decorate your bedroom with sharply contrasting colors. Instead, use softly complementary colors.

Don't use clock radios with red numbers, as these emanate unhealthy sha energy that can disturb your rest.

Do use light green linens on your bed if you want more children.

179

Do tie a white ribbon imprinted with red hearts around pictures of, or letters from, your sweetheart.

Do choose clock radios with white or green numbers, as they don't 3:23 radiate harmful negative energy.

Don't put electronic equipment such as computers and fax machines in your bedroom.

Do cleanse and dust your crystals often to keep them sparkling.

183

Do decorate with chandeliers and crystal lights in the SW part of your home.

Don't hang wind chimes in your bedroom or office, as they're meant to be used outdoors. Instead, use quartz or amethyst crystals as enhancements for bringing support to your endeavors.

Do hang pink or red crystal hearts in the SW area of each room of your home.

Do decorate
with a statue of a
Chinese unicorn in
your dining room—
his chi represents
happiness.

Do frame and hang love poetry in the dining room, family room, or bedroom.

Do pay attention to seating at the dinner parties you host.

Do use a round dining table (instead of a square or rectangular one) to avoid seating a guest at one of its corners.

Don't place a seat under an exposed beam at your dining room table, for beams always represent separation from another person.

191

Do choose a home that has more doors than windows so that you'll keep the upper hand over your children.

Do put a picture of your mother in a porcelain frame. Motherhood is symbolized by the element of earth, which is represented by porcelain and china.

Do accessorize with earth materials and colors in the NE and SW.

Do wear rose quartz jewelry on your left arm to attract love.

Do place stone or porcelain statues or figurines of couples in the NW corners of rooms.

Do place a rose quartz heart near the picture of your intended loved one to activate affection and intention.

Do use stone statues of cherubs in the SW part of your garden, as they match the element for this direction and strengthen its effect.

Do place a pair of carved rose quartz hearts under each pillow of your bed.

Do decorate with earth materials such as clay, terra cotta, or porcelain in the SW areas of your rooms.

Do have pictures of family groups in the E.

Do use a black lacquer or wooden picture frame for a photo of your brothers and sisters.

Do add blue and black, both representing water, to the E to increase harmony in your home.

Do place paintings of bamboo and plums together in the E to represent a couple.

Do put wooden garden furniture in the E part of your garden for family harmony.

Do grow vegetables, herbs, and medicinal plants in the E part of your garden.

Do your morning exercises facing the E, from where the sun and its pure energy originates.

Do add a stuffed white or yellow tiger, or a tiger figurine, to the W in your family room.

Do put something that belonged to your dad in the NW part of your family room.

Do frame and hang the Chinese character for "Love" in the dining room, family room, or bedrooms.

210

Do introduce more green in your family room (for harmony).

211

Do put an amethyst quartz cluster in the family room.

Don't put any fertility symbols in the bathroom, as their effectiveness will be "flushed out" along with the waste water.

Do add a rocking chair to the W area of your bedroom.

Do buy an elephant statue and rub its forehead for fertility luck.

Do decorate the
SW corner of every
room with fire or
earth, red or
yellow, or things
in pairs.

Do decorate with magnolias, as they symbolize a happy marriage.

Don't keep wilting flowers in your home.

Do use floral images sparingly in your bedroom.

Do use images of two red roses in the SW to represent the love between you and your partner.

Do use images of apples in your home if you want to attract a beautiful woman into your life.

Do decorate with images of apricots, as they represent beautiful women.

Do hang paintings of fruits—especially apples, pomegranates, or persimmons—in your dining room or bedrooms.

223

Do change the position of bedroom furniture following illness, divorce, or the death of your partner.

Do use any bedroom over a garage as a guest room.

Do create a romantic seating or lounging area in the SW zone of your garden.

Do put large boulders, or plant trees or tall hedges, in the NW area of your garden to bring your father's love to you.

Do use wood trellises and arbors in the E area of your garden. Wood is the element of youth, family, and harmony.

Do add stone benches in the SW and NE areas of your garden.

Do install outdoor lights in the S and SW areas of your garden to give your relationship and romance more "fuel."

230

Do decorate with a geode or crystal cluster if you love learning.

Do decorate with framed posters about love, family, and marriage in the center of your home.

Do place two carved rose quartz hearts in the SW area of your rooms.

Do be aware that when you move in with someone else, your energy changes the existing environment of the dwelling.

Do an aggressive cleaning of your new home, especially if a divorced couple previously owned it.

Do activate the interests-outside-your-home-area (the NW) with metal symbols. Remember that, be it at the health-and-fitness center or a university class, there are new acquaintances to be made.

Do choose a home in which the master bedroom is behind the center horizontal line of the house. This provides a heightened sense of safety and security for you.

237

Don't choose a home in which the master bedroom is in the front of the house facing the street. It should be protected in the rear.

Do avoid decorating and using synthetic materials in your home as much as possible.

239

Don't limit your thinking, but think in terms of yin and yang, sun and moon, earth and heaven, mountains and water.

Don't choose a home that has the corner of another home or building pointing directly at the front door.

241

Don't choose a home in a cul-de-sac that receives the beams of car headlights aimed at it.

Don't live in a home with a toilet, kitchen, or bathroom in the SW area.

243

Do keep balance of yin (dark, soft, curves) and yang (light, hard, straight lines) in your home.

Don't change your residence if you're pregnant, for you may dislodge the vital energy that converged at conception.

Don't buy or live in an L-shaped house with the missing area in the SW— this indicates that the relationship area is absent.

Do choose a home that's basically square or rectangular in shape, as those shapes represent balance in all aspects of your life.

Don't bring antique jewelry into your home until after you've cleansed its energy. You can do this by passing the item through the smoke of your favorite incense. (This process is known as smudging.)

Do wear jewelry from a beloved parent, mentor, or friend to keep the person's spirit with you while you're apart.

Do wear jewelry with your birthstone for protection and personal empowerment.

Do use earth tones such as yellows, reds, and tans in your SW-area kitchen to block the turbulence in the love area.

Don't design your home so that a kitchen is in the exact center of the house; instead, it should be toward the earth areas of NE or SW. This will help you feel more centered.

Don't hang ceremonial swords, knives, sabers, or other sharp instruments in a bedroom—they send out killing energy.

Don't give a set of knives or scissors as a wedding or birthday gift, for it may sever your friendship.

Do keep the lighting soft, warm, and low by your bed.

Do hang a picture of a Chinese unicorn *(chi ling)* in your living room, as it represents a big family with lots of children.

Do use a painting of an even number of swans in the living room.

257

Don't put a tabletop water element in the S area of your living room, for the water will destroy the fire of the S—and happiness along with it.

Do add images of the Chinese love flowers—narcissus and orchids—to your living room.

Don't let masculine interests and art dominate your home if you're a man, but rather, add female images to attract females into your life.

Do add the fragrance of jasmine to your life, as it represents the female presence.

Do create a good balance of soft and hard surfaces and textures around you.

Do set up your ancestral altar in your living room.

263

Do display two roses in a vase in your living room, dining room, or bedroom to bring love into those areas of your home.

264

Do move pictures of a dead spouse or partner into the family or living room to allow a new relationship into your life.

265

Do use two metal cranes as statues or fountain-heads in your garden pond, for they represent long life, the prerequisite to a long marriage or relationship!

Do use a ceramic or metal picture frame for a photo of your father. These two elements create and support the relationship between the two of you.

Do hang seven pictures of babies or children in metal frames if you want to add to your family.

Do suspend a multifaceted round crystal over your telephone to activate its ringing more often.

Don't install metal benches, railings, or arbors in the E part of your garden. The element of metal destroys the harmony and family life that's represented by E's element of wood.

Don't store metal equipment in the E part of your garden, as it will destroy family harmony.

Don't use any mirrored surfaces (such as a gazing ball) in the E part of your yard.

Don't have any mirrors in the bedroom that reflect the occupants of the bed. Mirrors will energize rather than calm down your energy, thus disturbing a restful sleep.

273

Do use a mirror to reflect the view of any corners from your neighbor's house or garage, which is visible from your pillow.

Do keep your mirrors bright and clean.

275

Do face a mirror toward unpleasant neighbors to deflect the negative energy originating from them.

Do position your ancestral altar against a N wall so that it acts as a mountain supporting your family.

277

Do enhance the NW area with earth materials such as clay, terra cotta, and stone to enhance the possibility of fatherhood.

Don't remove any tall trees or hedges from the NW area of your yard—these represent the male head of the household and protection for your family.

Do hang wind chimes with two or six rods in the living room, family room, or kitchen.

Don't buy or live in an L-shaped house that has a missing NW corner. This represents long absences of a husband, father, or male partner.

Do hang pictures of places you want to travel to or things you love to do in the NW to open up the possibility of meeting new people.

Don't have three people in a photograph in the SW romance area. This odd number represents an interloper in a relationship.

Do put things only in multiples of two in the SW to create the powerful pairing energy of couples.

Don't use a grouping of three candles, as this upsets the harmony of a romantic relationship.

Do tie two red or purple ribbons on your bedroom doorknob if you want to attract romance into your life.

Do keep your accessories in twos to stimulate the yin and yang energies.

Do display a pair of doves in the love area of your rooms, as they mate for life.

Do tuck two crystal hearts under your pillow.

289

Do display
photos of long
and happily
married couples
in your home.

Do place a photo of your mother and daughter (or grandmother) in the SW to strengthen their bonds to each other.

Do keep
photos of
your father
in the NW.

Don't overdecorate with too many masculine *or* feminine symbols and images; rather, keep a balance of both.

293

Don't adorn your home with morbid, depressing, or lewd images.

Do hang a framed picture of 100 children if you want more children in your life.

Do put photo-
graphs of pines
and junipers in
the NW.

296

Do put travel posters in your NW area. Many couples have met through tours, cruises, and trips.

Don't use dried flowers, plants, or grasses as decoration in your bedroom.

298

Don't place any plants in the center—they represent the wood element, which destroys the earth element of the "heart" of your home.

Do decorate with porcelain-framed love sonnets.

Don't put a pond to the right of your front door (looking out), as it will bring another person into your relationship.

Do deflect the killing energy of the roofline or corner of a neighboring house with a small round or octagonal mirror.

Do use a flat screen to hide your desk or work space from your bed.

Do bend a hinged screen so that no acute or sharp angles create sha energy pointed toward your bed.

Do use linen sprays and scents on your sheets and blankets during use and storage.

Do

Do use the aromas of geranium and orange to enhance love and romance in your home.

Do use perfumed soaps, powders, and scents that make you feel sensual, especially at bedtime.

307

Do mist your home with the scent of pine to attract long-term friendships.

308

Do enjoy a cluster of nine candles in the S area of any room for happiness.

Do hang an embroidered red ball in the S or SW corner as a symbol of marriage.

Do use triangles and pyramids in the S to increase joy.

Do place images of pheasants or phoenixes in the S of any room to bring more joy and happiness.

Don't put water elements such as fountains or aquariums in the S, as they douse the fire of celebration and happiness.

Do place a heavy piece of furniture in the most yang (S) part of your new home when you move in.

Do have photos of your mother or grandmother in the SW so their spirits will support and guide you.

Do have photos of you and your sweetheart in a heart-shaped frame in the SW.

Do put something that reminds you of or belonged to Mom or Grandma in the SW. Such mementos will comfort you in their absence. (You can also wear jewelry or clothing you inherited from them.)

Do decorate with pairs of hearts in the SW area of your bedroom.

Do put porcelain figurines representing love in the SW.

Do accessorize with red and purple in the SW to activate relationships.

320

Do add reds, purples, and yellows to the SW areas of your rooms and house as a whole.

Do use clay and ceramic tiles and plant containers in the SW areas of your house and garden.

Do display pictures of mother and child(ren) in the SW to strengthen their attachment.

Do place a figurine of a bride and groom in your SW.

Do use a figurine of two doves in your SW relationship area, for they represent long life and faithfulness.

Don't choose a house with a toilet in the SW relationship area.

Don't choose a house with the SW relationship area missing, as this represents the absence of love, marriage, or motherhood from your life.

Do place solid furniture (not on thin legs or wobbly) in the S and SW areas of each room.

Do place books about love and relationships in the SW corner of each room.

Do use romantic images (such as Cupid) in any statuary in the SW areas of your rooms or garden.

Do store swords and other sharp weapons wrapped in red fabric with their points downward.

Do move the television from your bedroom into the family or other community room.

Do hide your television inside a closed cabinet or wardrobe if it's in the bedroom.

Do use another toilet if there's one located in the SW (relationship) area of your home—or it will weaken communication and support among your family members.

Don't have the head of your bed share a wall with a toilet or sink.

Do let go of your childhood—remove toys, stuffed animals, and the like from your bedroom.

Do paint your SW bedroom wall peach if you're a bachelorette who wants to attract a good relationship.

Do add lots of yellow to your SW bedroom wall if you want to become a parent. Yellow symbolizes the earth element of motherhood and the generating element of fatherhood (metal).

Don't position the side of your bed up against a wall. Leave space there.

Do minimize the use of patterned wall and window coverings and flooring in your bedroom.

Do balance the yin and yang throughout your home with dark and light.

341

Don't put an aquarium or fountain in the S area of any room—the water snuffs out contentment and satisfaction with life.

Do add a water feature such as a pond or waterfall in the E part of your yard.

Do use desktop fountains and images of water in the E to improve family togetherness.

344

Don't add a fountain, pond, or waterfall in the S in your garden.

345

Don't install a waterfall on the right (yin/female) side of your front door as you look out. It introduces another female or an interloper to the household.

Do activate the W (the children area) with white, metal, or earth objects if you wish to enlarge your family.

347

Don't have more windows than doors in your home, for this imbalance weakens your authority.

Do keep window coverings closed when you sleep at night.

349

Do put pictures of your siblings in wooden frames to surround them with the element of harmony.

Do put pictures of loving couples in wooden frames to keep the peace and affection between them and in their households.

Do decorate with pine trees and pine motifs, as they represent enduring relationships.

Do use wooden images of adult lovers and sweethearts in the E area of your bedroom.

Do add a wooden elephant, with its trunk curved up-ward, to the E. This is the symbol of a happy family unit.